WHAT MAKES A COMMUNITY?

SCHOOLS

by J. P. Press

Consultant: Marla Conn, Reading Specialist, Read-Ability

BEARPORT PUBLISHING

Minneapolis, Minnesota

Teaching Tips

Before Reading

- Look at the cover of the book. Discuss the picture and the title.
- Ask readers to brainstorm a list of what they already know about schools. What can they expect to see in this book?
- Go on a picture walk, looking through the pictures to discuss vocabulary and make predictions about the text.

During Reading

- Read for purpose. Encourage readers to think about the school and its role in the community as they are reading.
- Ask readers to think about the setting of the book. Where does the story take place?
- Ask readers to look for the details of the story. What is happening?
- If readers encounter an unknown word, ask them to look at the sounds in the word. Then, ask them to look at the rest of the page. Are there any clues to help them understand?

After Reading

- Encourage readers to pick a buddy and reread the book together.
- Ask readers to name three things from this book that they could find at a school. Go back and find the pages that tell about these things.
- Ask readers to write and draw a picture about something that they learned about the school.

Credits:
Cover and title page, © lawcain/iStock; 3, © Africa Studio/Shutterstock; 5, © martinedoucet/iStock; 6–7, © Chris Pearsall/Alamy Stock Photo; 8, © kali9/iStock; 10, © targovcom/iStock; 11, © FatCamera/iStock; 12, © New Africa/Shutterstock; 14–15, © Dmitry Bruskov/Shutterstock; 17, © TongRo Images/Alamy Stock Photo; 18, © Brian Eichhorn/Shutterstock; 20–21, © Monkey Business Images/Shutterstock; 22, © Monkey Business Images/Dreamstime; 23BL, © Viacheslav Lopatin/Shutterstock; 23BM, © FatCamera/iStock; 23BR, © charmphoto/Shutterstock; 23TL, © MikeDotta/Shutterstock; 23TM, © Chinnapong/iStock; 23TR, © Minerva Studio/Shutterstock

Library of Congress Cataloging-in-Publication Data

Names: Press, J. P., 1993– author.
Title: Schools / J.P. Press.
Description: Minneapolis, Minnesota : Bearport Publishing Company, [2021] |
Series: What makes a community? | Includes bibliographical references
and index.
Identifiers: LCCN 2020029788 (print) | LCCN 2020029789 (ebook) | ISBN
9781647474492 (library binding) | ISBN 9781647474577 (paperback) | ISBN
9781647474652 (ebook)
Subjects: LCSH: Schools—Juvenile literature.
Classification: LCC LB1556 .P74 2021 (print) | LCC LB1556 (ebook) | DDC
371—dc23
LC record available at https://lccn.loc.gov/2020029788
LC ebook record available at https://lccn.loc.gov/2020029789

Copyright © 2021 Bearport Publishing Company. All rights reserved. No part of this publication may be reproduced in whole or in part, stored in any retrieval system, or transmitted in any form or by any means, electronic, mechanical, photocopying, recording, or otherwise, without written permission from the publisher.

For more information, write to Bearport Publishing, 5357 Penn Avenue South, Minneapolis, MN 55419.

Printed in the United States of America.

Contents

A Day at School

Ring!

Do you hear the school bell?

It is time for school.

Let's go!

We start the day in our classroom.

Our teacher meets us at the door.

We are ready to learn!

We read books and do math.

RESPECT
Hello, Goodbye

Then, we visit other places in the school.

Some days we go to the gym.

Our **PE** teacher helps us stay healthy.

We sing songs in the music room.

Some days we play drums, too.

The art room is fun to visit.

What will you make?

We are hungry.

Let's go to the **cafeteria**.

The lunch workers give us our food.

Mmm.

It looks tasty!

After lunch, it is time to play.

There is so much to do on the **playground**.

We can swing.

We can go down the slide.

Shh!

We need to be quiet when we visit the **library**.

Look at all the books.

Do you feel sick?

You may need to see the **nurse**.

Go to the nurse's **office**.

You will feel better soon!

The bell rings again.

It is the end of the day.

Time to go home!

That was a great
day at school.

At the School

Glossary

cafeteria a place where people get food and eat

library a place where people can go to use or borrow books

nurse a person who takes care of people who are sick or hurt

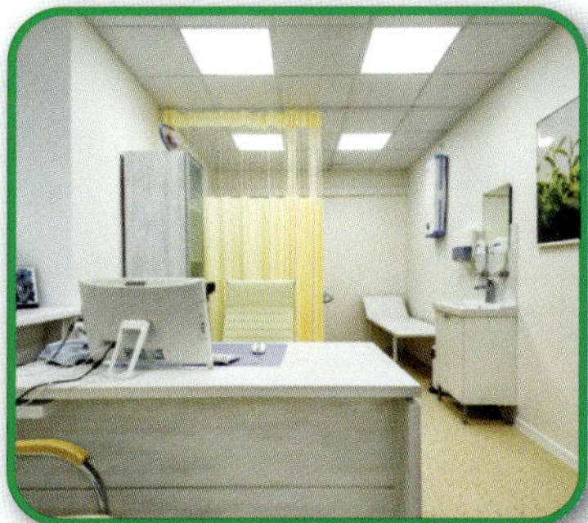

office a room where a person works

PE sports and exercise taught in schools

playground an area used for games and playing

Index

Read More

Emminizer, Theresa. *You're Part of a School Community! (All Our Communities).* New York: Gareth Stevens, 2020.

Leaf, Christina. *Teachers (Blastoff! Readers. Community Helpers).* Minneapolis: Bellwether Media, 2021.

Learn More Online

1. Go to **www.factsurfer.com**
2. Enter "**Schools Community**" into the search box.
3. Click on the cover of this book to see a list of websites.

About the Author

J. P. Press likes to run, read, and help her community any way she can! She knows a lot of great teachers.